PYRAMID

PYRAMID

DAVID MACAULAY

HOUGHTON MIFFLIN COMPANY BOSTON

To My Parents

Special thanks to Janice, without whose help this book would
never have been finished, and to Ed Brovarski, Curatorial Assistant
of the Egyptian Department at the Boston Museum of Fine Arts,
for time freely given and encouragement gratefully received.

Also Available in Sandpiper Paperbound Edition:

CATHEDRAL: The Story of Its Construction

Library of Congress Cataloging in Publication Data

Macaulay, David.
　Pyramid.

　SUMMARY: Text and black-and-white illustrations
follow the intricate step-by-step process of the
building of an ancient Egyptian pyramid.
　1. Pyramids — Construction — Juvenile literature.
|1. Pyramids.　2. Egypt — Civilization|　I. Title.
DT63.M25　　690′.6′8　　75-9964
ISBN 0-395-21407-6

Life in ancient Egypt was fairly simple. Most people were farmers. For eight or nine months of the year they tended their small plots of land along the Nile river, growing wheat, fruit, and vegetables. Others raised cattle, sheep, and goats. They tried to feed themselves, pay their taxes, and store enough food to last through the annual inundation. This was the time between July and November when the river rose and flooded most of the farmland. The water eventually receded, leaving a new layer of rich and fertile earth.

Between 3000 and 1100 BC the country was ruled by a long line of kings called pharaohs. Under the pharaohs were members of the royal court, governors of the provinces into which the land was divided, and commanders of the army. Priests and priestesses who officiated at religious ceremonies and attended the many gods that the Egyptians worshiped also served under the pharaohs.

Egypt consisted of two narrow strips of farmland which lined both banks of the Nile from Aswan in the south to the Delta in the north. East and west of the farmland lay hundreds of square miles of desert. This geography created a dependence on the river that insured efficient communication throughout the land and made complete control by the pharaoh and his army a relatively easy task.

Death in ancient Egypt was considered the beginning of a new life in another world. This life, assuming certain precautions were taken, would last forever. Because life on earth was relatively short, the Egyptians built their houses of mud. They built their tombs of stone since life after death was eternal.

The Egyptians believed that besides a physical body everyone had a soul called a ba and a spiritual duplicate of themselves called a ka. When the body died an individual's ba continued to live here on earth, resting within the body at night. His or her ka, on the other hand, traveled back and forth between the earth and the other world. Eternal life depended on both the ba and the ka being able to identify the body. For this reason corpses were preserved by the process of mummification.

The tomb into which a body was placed had two main functions. It was designed to protect the body from the elements and from thieves who might try to steal the gold and precious objects placed in and around the coffin and it also had to serve as a house for the ka. The more important the person, the greater his tomb. Since at death pharaohs became gods, their tombs were the largest and most elaborate of all.

Between 2700 and 2200 BC royal tombs were surrounded by a complex of temples and smaller tombs called mastabas. The burial chamber of the king was protected by a manmade mountain of stone called a pyramid. Its four triangular sides spreading below a single peak represented the rays of the sun shining down over the pharaoh, linking him directly and for all time to Re, the god of the sun. A temple containing a false door through which the ka traveled was built against the east side of the pyramid. All burial grounds were located on the west bank of the Nile since it was in the west that the sun set, beginning its nightly journey into the other world — the same journey that the ka had to make.

The pyramid and complex of surrounding temples and tombs in this story are imaginary. They are, however, based closely on several of the pyramids and remnants of temples still standing in Egypt. It is generally agreed that earth ramps were used in the construction process but there is a difference of opinion as to where those ramps were constructed in relation to the pyramid. I have included the two most popular theories in the way that I see them most satisfactorily employed. Although the pyramids failed, in fact, to protect their burial chambers from robbers they succeeded in making their creators immortal. The pyramids continue to serve as a tribute to those who so skillfully organized the efforts of thousands of people in an attempt to deny the finality of death and the limitations of time by leaving behind something that would last forever.

In 2470 BC a new pharaoh of upper and lower Egypt was crowned. The coronation took place in Memphis, the city from which he would rule for thirty-one years. Earlier pharaohs, including his father, had established the supremacy of Egypt over her neighbors. The military and spiritual supremacy of the pharaoh at home was unquestioned. His soldiers traveled the length of the Nile collecting taxes and keeping a watchful eye over the local governors.

Within two years the pharaoh began preparing for the end of his life on earth and the beginning of his eternal life as a god. Accordingly, he instructed Mahnud Hotep, his architect and best friend, to design a tomb for him that would stand for all time.

Even before the plans were complete, a site was chosen on the west bank of the Nile. It was a high plateau overlooking the valley. A few miles to the south stood the great funerary complex at Giza where the pyramids of three earlier pharaohs could be seen. Out of respect to Khufu, the builder of the largest of the Giza pyramids, the pharaoh decreed that his pyramid should be only 470 feet high — ten feet lower than Khufu's. He compensated for his generosity, however, by choosing a site twenty feet higher than the plateau at Giza.

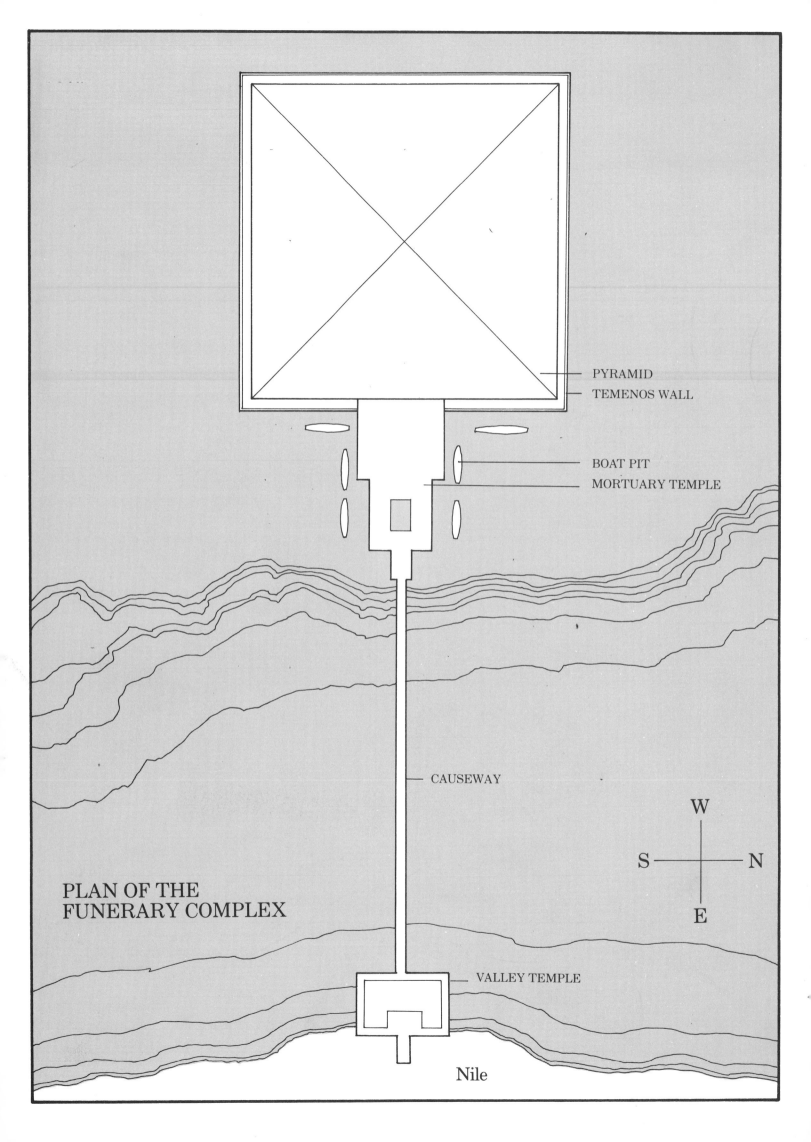

PYRAMID

TEMENOS WALL

BOAT PIT

MORTUARY TEMPLE

CAUSEWAY

W

S —— N

E

PLAN OF THE
FUNERARY COMPLEX

VALLEY TEMPLE

Nile

Within two months a plan for a complex similar to Giza was finished and presented to the pharaoh. The largest structure was the pyramid, which covered the tomb. To the east stood the mortuary temple in which the pharaoh's ka would sometimes dwell. Extending from both sides of the mortuary temple and enclosing the area around the base of the pyramid was a wall called the temenos wall. Farther to the east on the banks of the river stood the valley temple to which the body of the pharaoh would be first brought. The temples were connected by an enclosed passage called the causeway. Large oblong pits were also shown in which the pharaoh's funerary boats were to be buried.

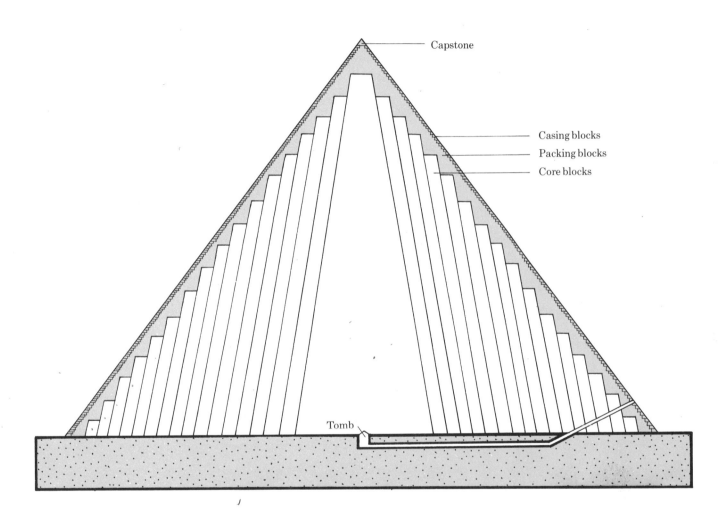

The pyramid itself had three main parts. The innermost section was the step-like central core. Only the facing blocks of each sloping band of the core were carefully finished. Second were the packing blocks, which rested on the steps around the core. They were carefully cut and fitted. Third were the outer casing blocks laid against the packing stones. These were of the highest quality and were cut with greater care and precision than any of the others. All three parts were constructed simultaneously, one course or layer at a time.

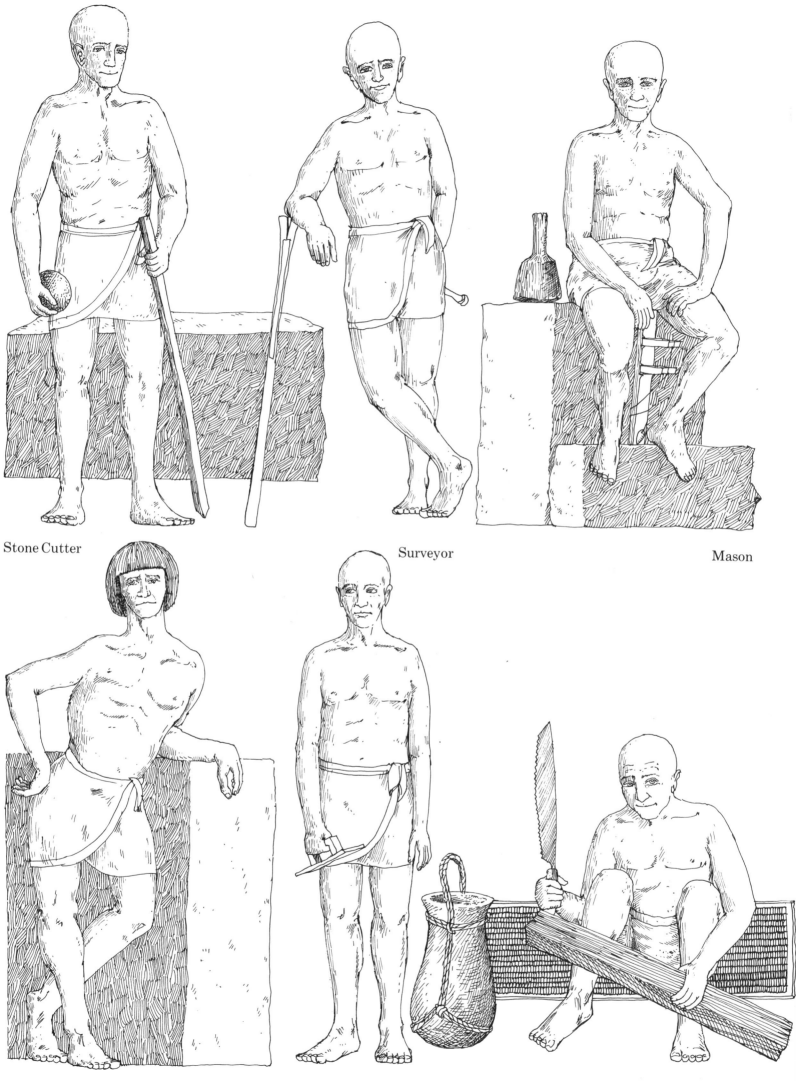

Stone Cutter

Surveyor

Mason

Foreman

Mortar Maker

Carpenter

As the plans were being drawn up, several thousand men, including stone-cutters, masons, surveyors, mortar makers, carpenters, and general laborers were brought to the area. They would work all year long either in the quarries or on the site. Barracks and workshops were built at both locations. A larger work force of over fifty thousand men, most of them farmers, was also drafted every year between July and November when the fields were flooded and farming was impossible. They were organized into gangs to transport stone from the quarries to the site. Each gang consisted of twenty-five men, including a soldier who was the foreman. All the men were paid in food and clothing.

Chisels

Mallet

Dolerite Ball

Polishing Stones

Trowel

Hammer

Square

Level

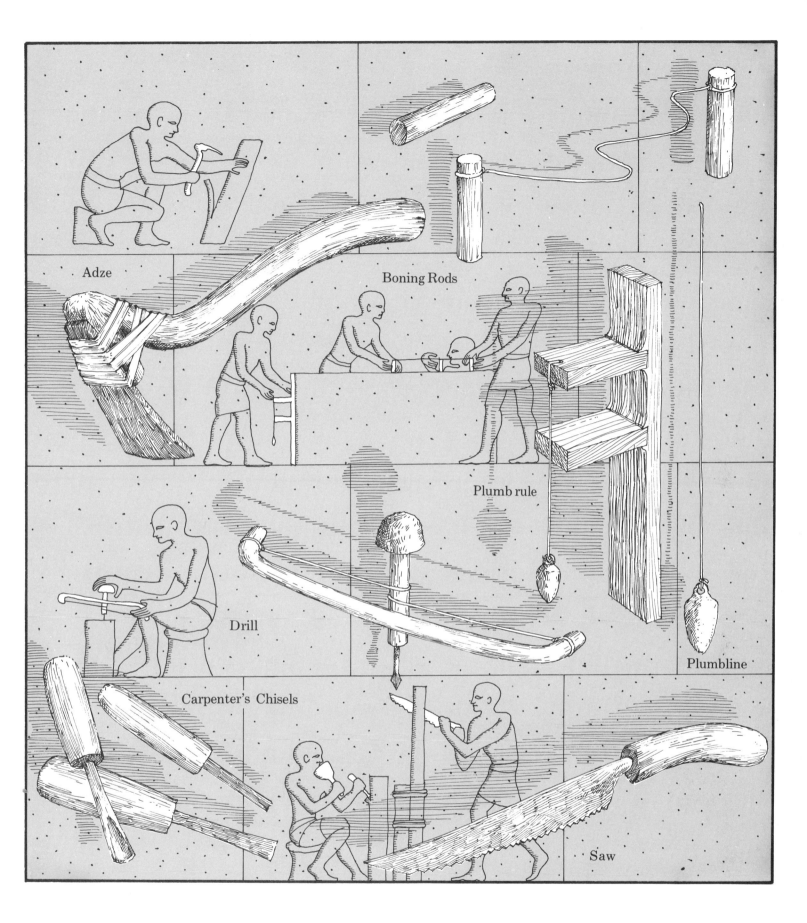

Adze

Boning Rods

Plumb rule

Drill

Carpenter's Chisels

Plumbline

Saw

Most of the tools the workmen would use for cutting stone were either made of copper or a very hard stone called dolerite. Handles for tools and most of the measuring instruments were made of wood. Metalworkers were kept busy both at the quarry and on the site sharpening worn tools and manufacturing new ones.

As soon as the plan was approved, Mahnud Hotep ordered the site cleared of sand and rubble in order to expose the rock on which the structures would be built.

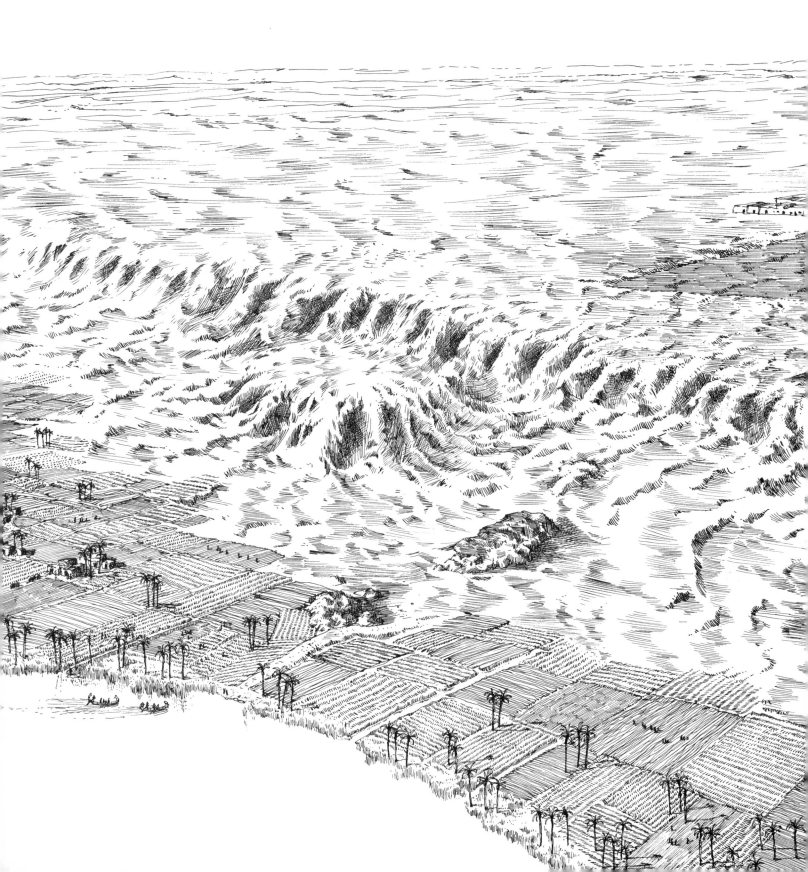

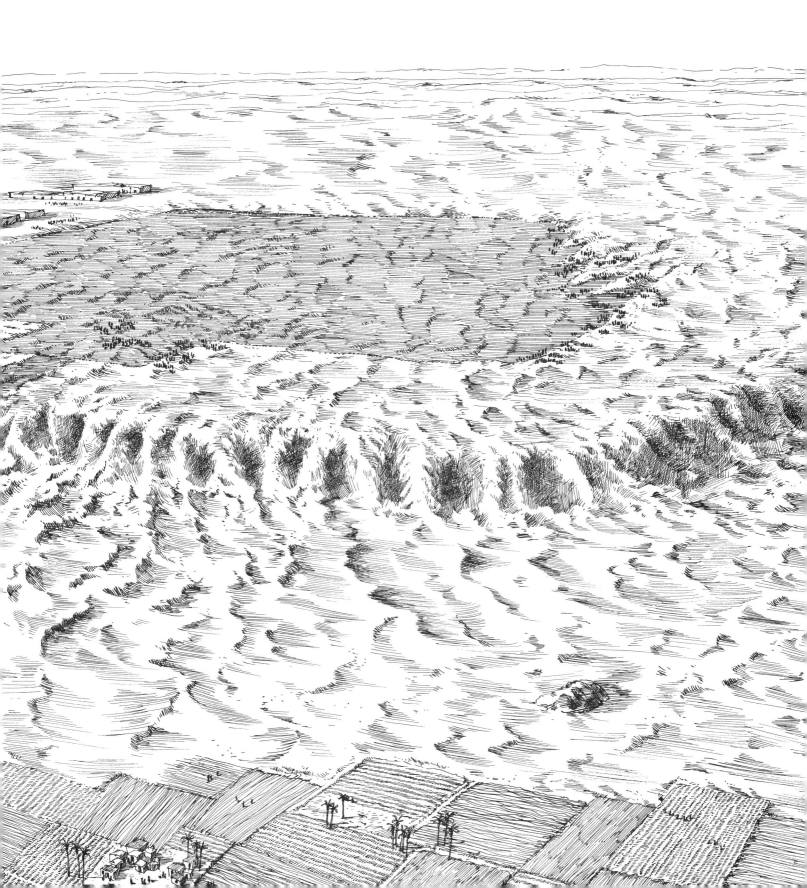

At the same time his scribes prepared a list of the necessary stone, giving the amount needed and the size for each block. Copies were sent to the quarries along with orders to begin work. Most of the stone used in the pyramid was limestone and much of it came from the area around the site. The better-quality stone, however, was quarried across the river at Tura. During the inundation most of this distance could be traveled by water, making the transportation of the heavy stones much easier.

To obtain the best limestone, tunnels were dug into the face of the cliffs from which huge caverns were cut block by block. Columns of stone were left standing in the caverns to support the roofs. As each block was cut it was assigned to a work gang for delivery. Using ropes and heavy timber levers the men would first roll the block onto a wooden sled and tie it down.

Then they dragged it to a waiting boat along a row of parallel logs embedded in the sand to prevent the runners of the sled from sinking under the weight.

All the stones were marked with the name of the work gang that hauled them and checked off the list when they reached the site.

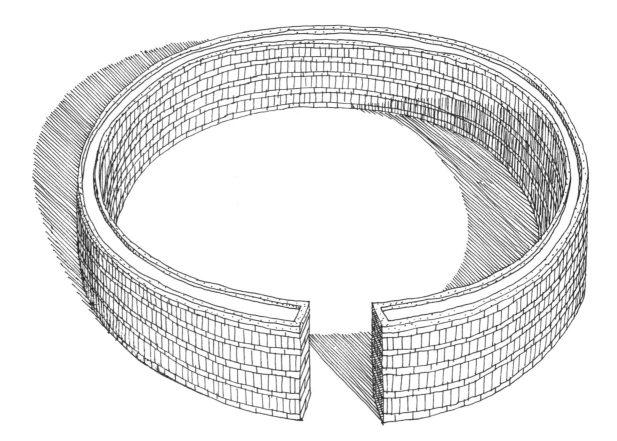

Before the building process could begin, the location of true north had to be determined, so that the pyramid could be accurately oriented. A circular wall was built approximately in the center of the site. It was built high enough to block a view of the surrounding hills and the top was made level. This created a perfect horizon line.

In the evening a priest stood in the center of the circle and watched for the appearance of a star in the east. Its position was marked as it rose above the wall and a line was drawn from that point on the wall to the center of the circle. He watched the star as it moved in an arc through the sky and finally set in the west. As it dropped behind the wall its position was marked again and another line was drawn to the center of the circle. Because stars appear to rotate around the north pole, the priests knew that a third line drawn from the center of the circle through the center of the space between the first two lines would point directly north.

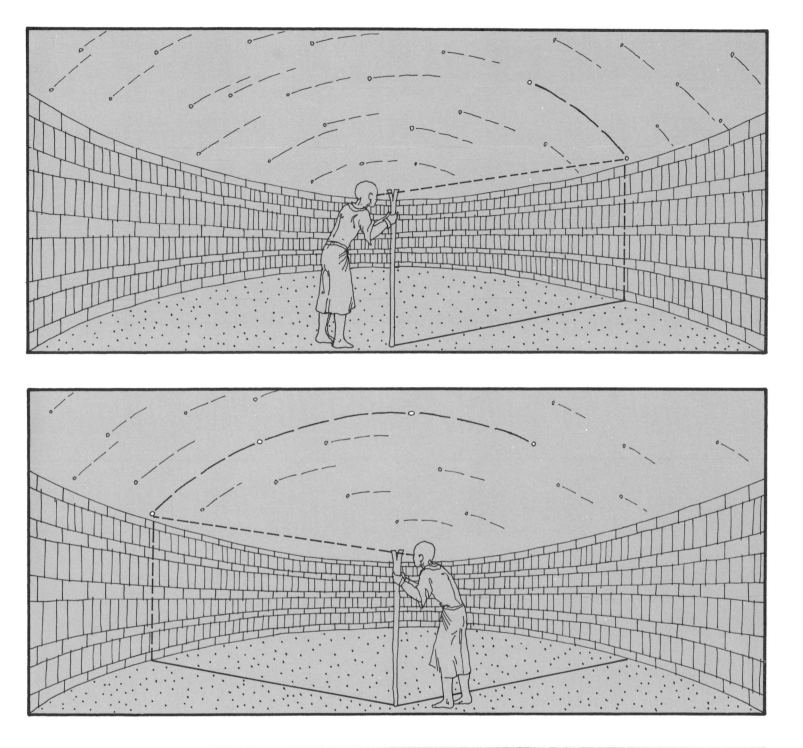
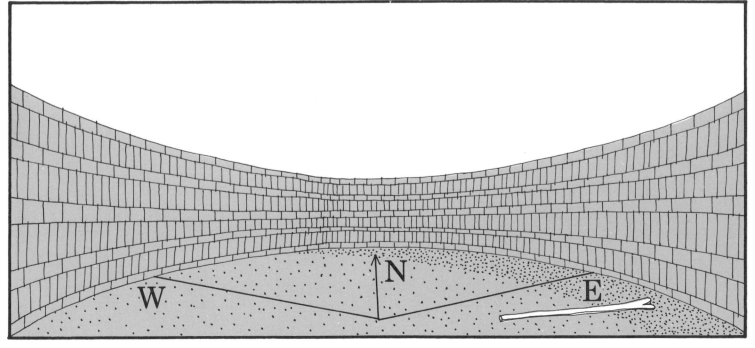

In November of 2468 the location of the pyramid was marked on the site by Mahnud Hotep and his surveyors. Several days later the process was symbolically repeated by the priests in the presence of the pharaoh. Each side of the pyramid was to be 740 feet long and metal stakes were driven into the rock at the four corners. For two weeks prayers were offered and several animals were sacrificed to the gods to ensure their blessings over the project.

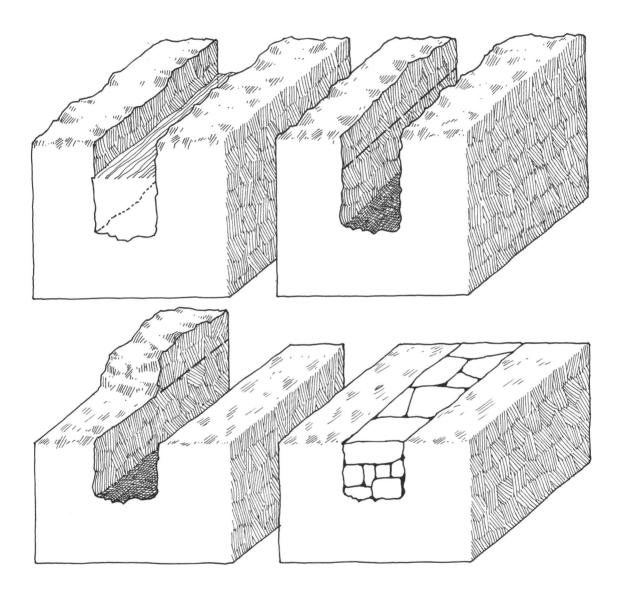

Before construction of the pyramid began the site was leveled. A network of narrow connecting trenches was cut into the rock over the entire area and filled with water, which acted as a level. When the top of the water had been marked on the sides of all the trenches they were drained. The spaces between the trenches were then cut down to the height of the marks and the trenches themselves filled with stone.

The site of the mortuary temple was also leveled and became a work area for the stonecutters. Next the foundation of the valley temple and causeway were constructed. The former served as an unloading dock while the latter became a ramp for dragging up the stones.

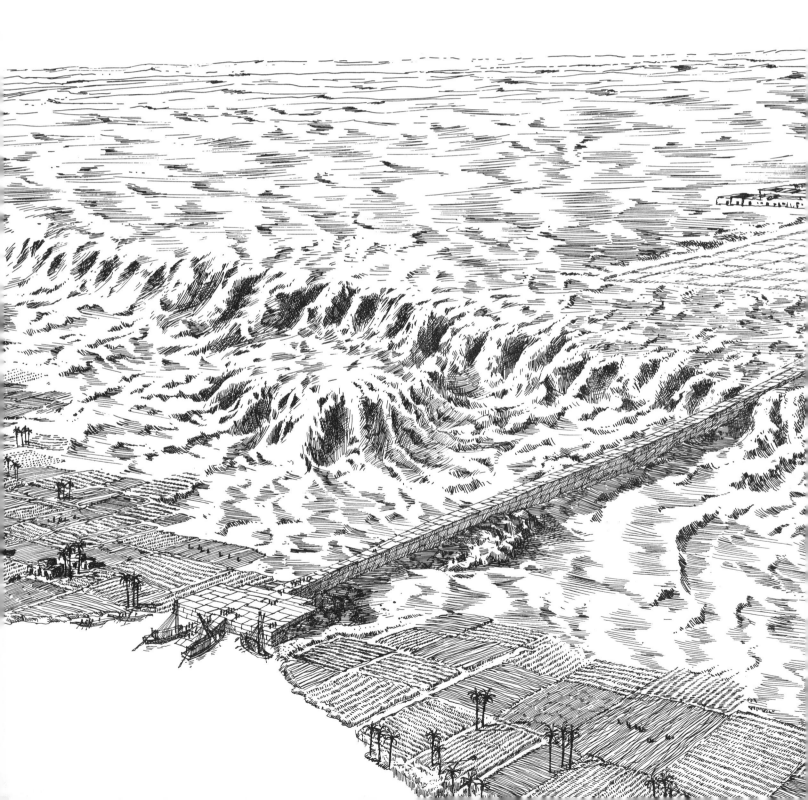

While the site was being leveled, work began on the passage to the tomb. Workers pounded their way through the rock using balls of dolerite. They were followed by men with chisels who carefully finished the four faces of the gradually descending shaft.

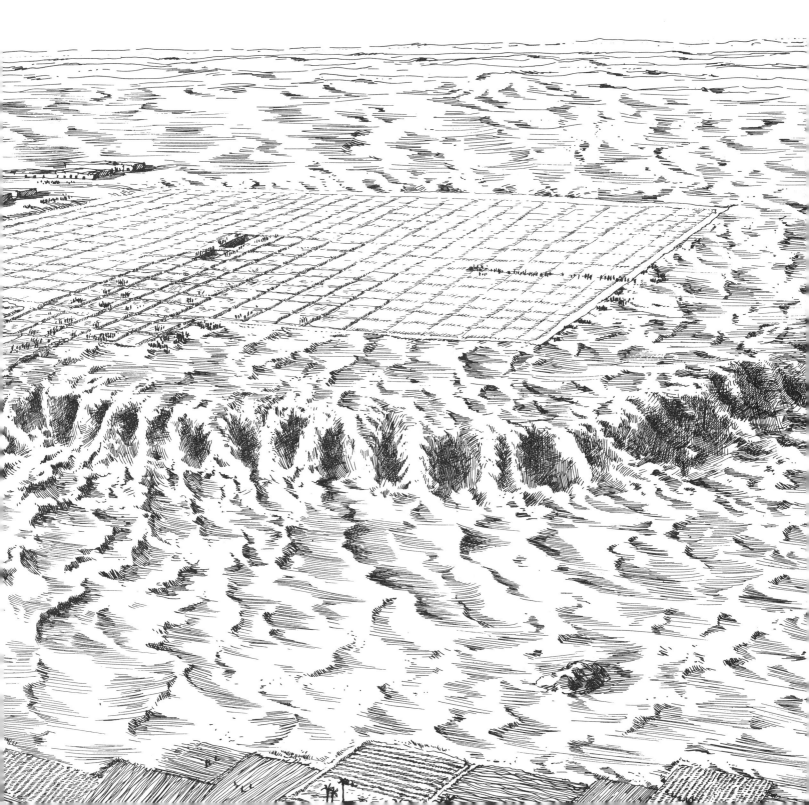

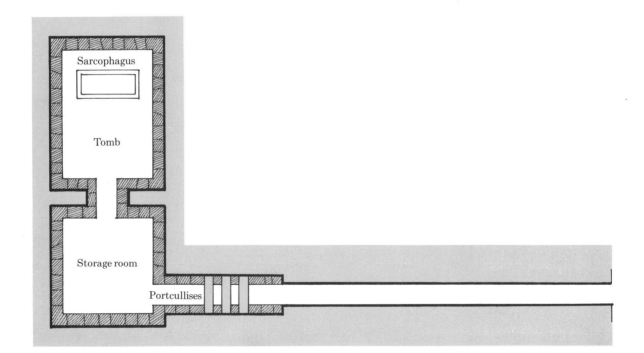

Upon reaching a level fifteen feet below the surface, the passage continued as a narrow horizontal corridor at the end of which two rooms were cut. The first would be used for storing the pharaoh's most important possessions. The second was the tomb itself. Both were dug down from the top and would eventually be roofed by massive granite slabs. Channels were built out from the walls of the tunnel, in which granite doors called portcullises were lowered to seal the rooms after the burial.

Granite was also used to line the inside of the rooms and to build the first fifteen courses of the casing. Most of this stone was cut from boulders found six hundred miles to the south in Aswan and ferried to the site on barges.

Huge blocks of both granite and limestone were dragged up the causeway to the work area and transferred onto more easily movable wooden rockers. After the tops and ends were chiseled smooth each stone was numbered in the order that it would be laid.

By September of 2467 the site had been leveled and many blocks were ready to be moved into place. Each one was rolled off its rocker onto several wooden logs standing over the approximate final location. After a thin coat of mortar had been smeared on the ends and bottom of a stone the logs were removed and it was pushed into place. First a row of carefully cut limestone paving stones was laid around the base line of the pyramid. Then the granite casing blocks of the first course were pushed into place along a line inscribed on top of the paving stones.

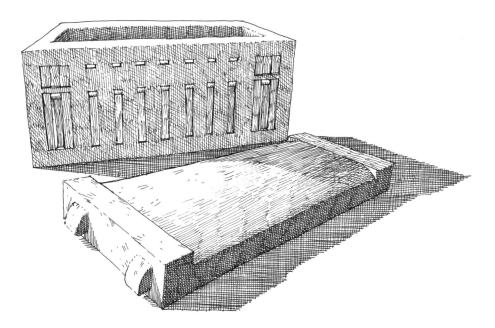

As the casing stones of the second course were being dragged into place work began on the roof over the inner rooms. Since the outer coffin or sarcophagus was too large to be brought through the tunnel it had to be placed in the burial chamber before the roof was built. First a wall was constructed to block the doorway between the two rooms and then the entire burial chamber was filled with sand and rubble. After the sarcophagus had been dragged into the center of the area, workmen tore down the wall and removed the fill. As the level of fill gradually dropped, the sarcophagus was carried down. When it rested safely on the floor the entire process was repeated to construct the roof.

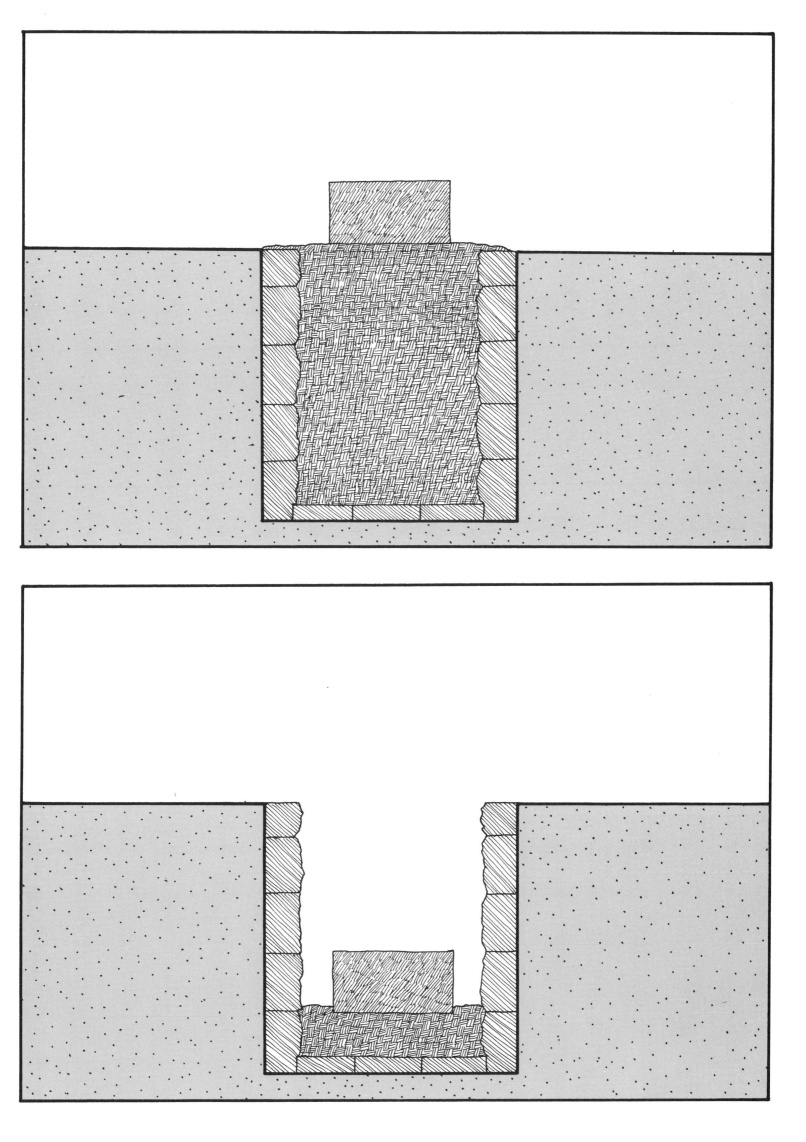

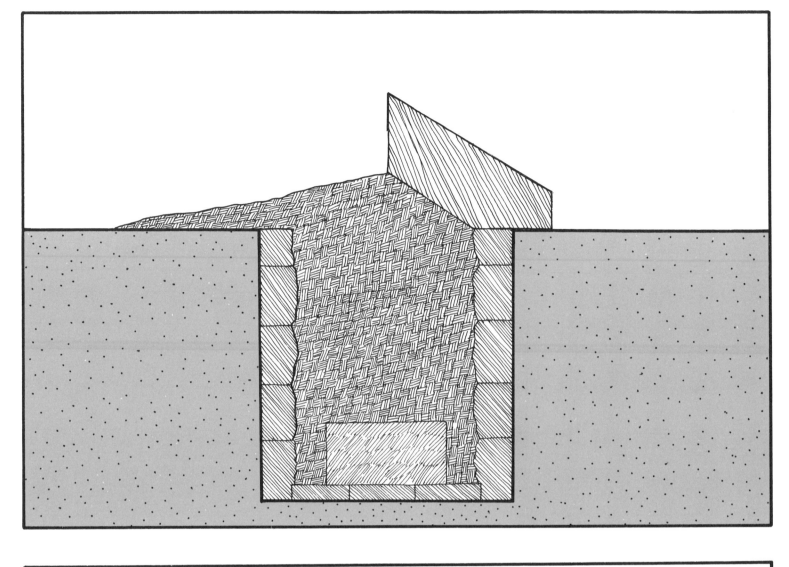

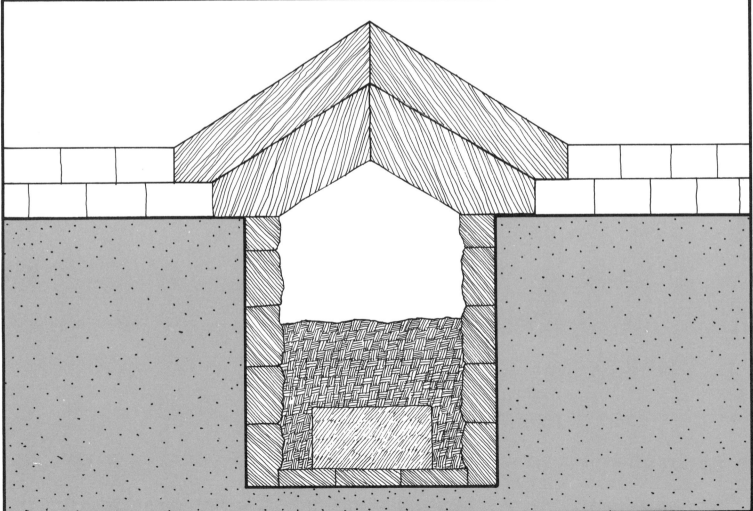

This time the rooms were both filled with earth formed into a mound that rose above the openings. Large granite slabs were dragged up both sides of the mound forming a peaked roof. Following careful inspection the earth was removed through the tunnel. Skilled stonecutters then finished the granite facing which lined the interior of the chambers.

The area enclosed by the casing stones was next filled with core and packing blocks and all the tops were leveled in preparation for the second course. Overseers checked the work constantly because any poorly finished surfaces could weaken the entire pyramid. By the following summer the first course was complete and all the stones for the second course had arrived.

Unlike the stones of the first course, which were moved into place fairly easily, the stones of the other 123 courses had to be raised to the top of the preceding course before they could be pushed into place. Mahnud Hotep solved this problem by building ramps of rubble held together with Nile mud. One ramp began at each corner of the pyramid and rose gradually along the side resting on the unfinished steps of the casing. Logs, embedded in the top of the ramp, helped reduce deterioration under the runners of the sleds. As each course was finished,

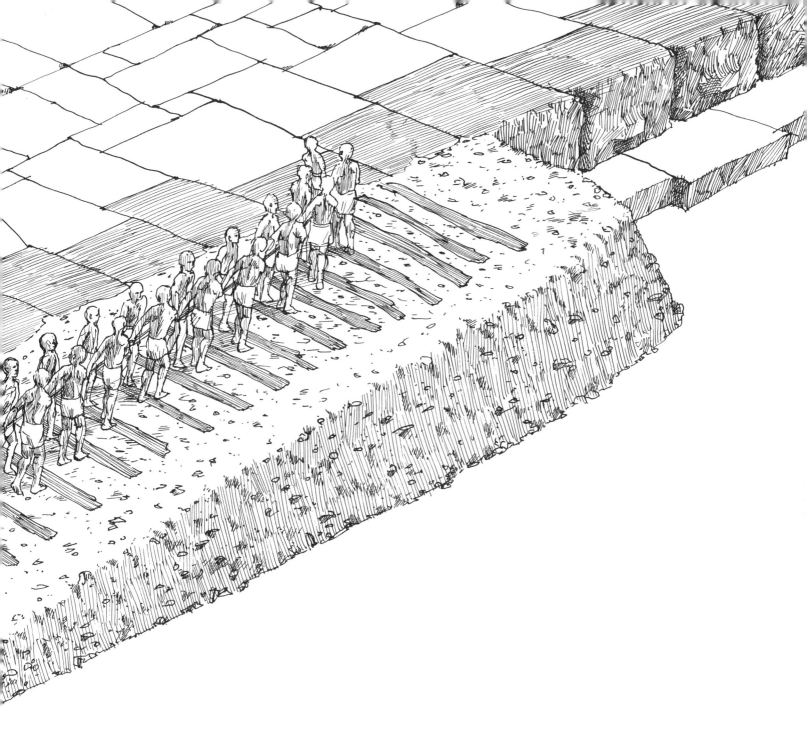

the ramps were extended by workmen whose job it was to build and maintain them.

As soon as the ramps were ready, work gangs began hauling the blocks for the second course into place. Usually twenty men pulled the sled while the others either pushed from behind with levers or poured liquid on the roadway to reduce friction under the runners.

As the base of the pyramid grew, the tunnel leading to the tomb was extended through it. The blocks over the roof of the tunnel were laid to form a peak like

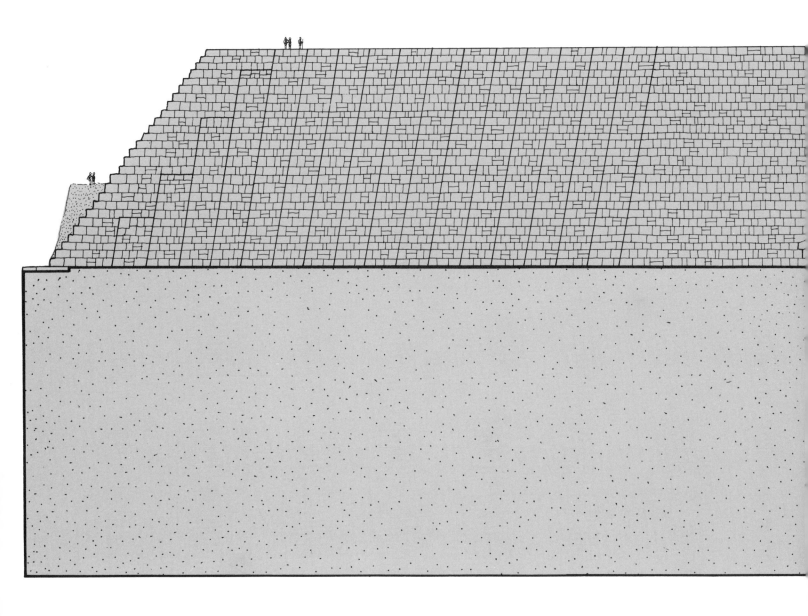

those over the inner chambers. By this method the enormous weight of the upper courses was directed around the tunnel.

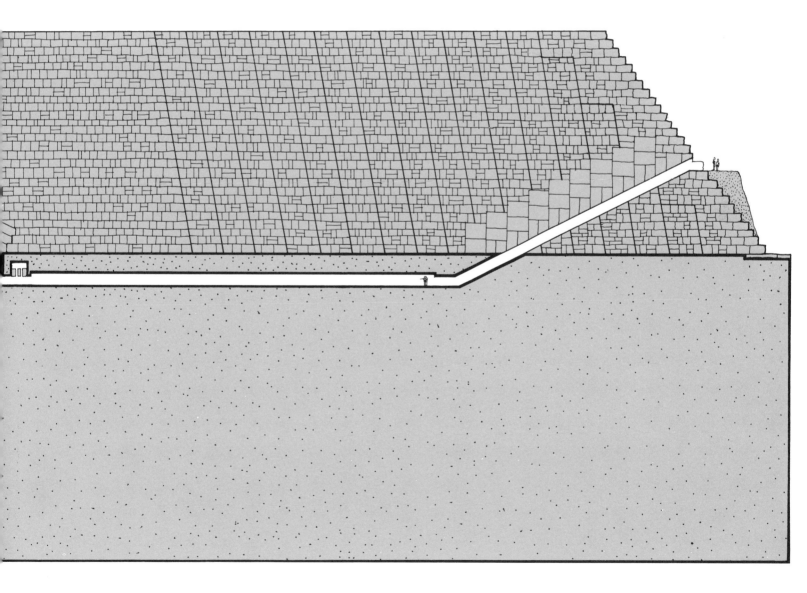

In the spring of 2461, the pharaoh instructed Mahnud Hotep to build a second smaller pyramid for his wife next to his own. Within weeks a site was cleared and the second royal tomb begun.

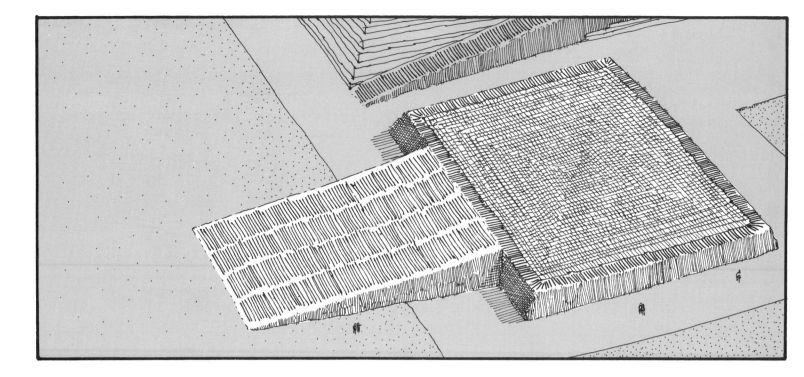

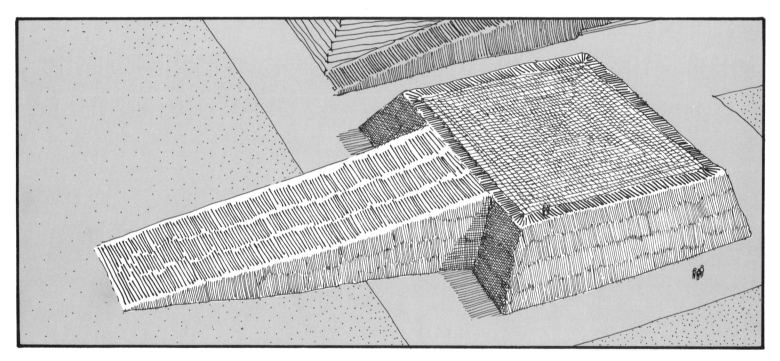

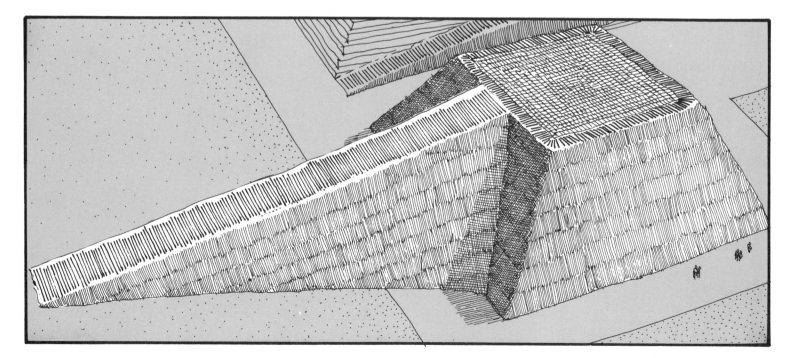

The Queen's pyramid was constructed in the same way as its larger neighbor but because of its size only a single ramp was necessary. It was built perpendicular to the south face while narrow banks of rubble and mud built around the other three sides made it easier for the workmen to move the casing stones into place.

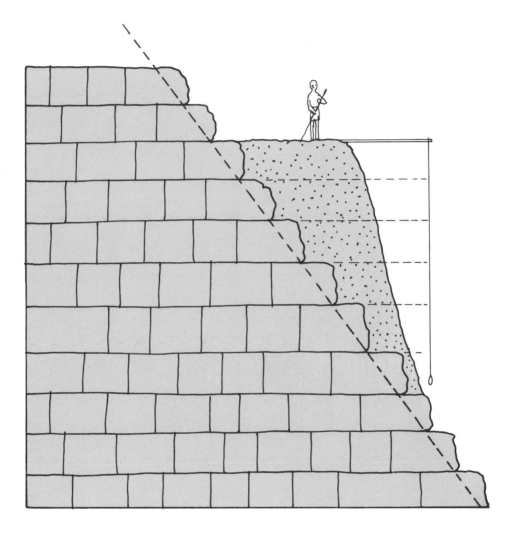

Besides checking the level of each course, the surveyors used plumblines to make sure that the walls of both pyramids were rising at the correct angle. As progress continued uninterrupted year after year, Mahnud Hotep's great ability as an organizer as well as an architect became obvious. From the beginning he had kept the quarries and work gangs far enough ahead of schedule to ensure that each block would be on the site when it was needed.

By winter of the tenth year the bases of both pyramids could easily be seen from fields several miles down the Nile. In the evenings as the farmers patched their mud houses or added extra rooms, they boasted about their years of service to the pharaoh and about the number of stones their gang had brought during the flood. But they and their families knew that in seven or eight months they would leave again, and there was always the possibility that they might not return. Accidents were quite common as the heavy stones were moved, and each year the villages lost several of their men.

In July of 2457 many of the work gangs were sent directly to the quarries at Tura where stones cut in the preceding months were waiting to be transported to the site. These were the fine white casing stones for the pharaoh's pyramid. For the next fourteen years boats sailed back and forth ferrying stone across the flooded valley. Thousands of blocks were dragged up the causeway, trimmed to size, and hauled up the ramps to their final destinations.

When the pyramid reached a height of four hundred feet there was no longer enough wall space to support all four ramps so two of them were abandoned. While a continuous procession of work gangs hauled their blocks up one of the remaining ramps the other was used for bringing the empty sleds back down.

As the pyramid grew higher, it also grew more quickly, and by October of 2442, twenty-six years after Mahnud Hotep first presented his plan, 124 courses had been completed. The flat area on top now measured only ten feet square.

On the first of November a special ceremony was held to mark the arrival of the granite capstone. This large block, which was cut roughly in the shape of a small pyramid, would rest on the top course. After numerous prayers and offerings it was dragged off the boat and up the causeway to the foot of one of the ramps. Following more prayers laborers began the long climb to the summit, hauling the block behind them. Another group with ropes and levers traveled behind to prevent the sled from sliding backward when the haulers rested and to help move the enormous weight around each corner of the pyramid.

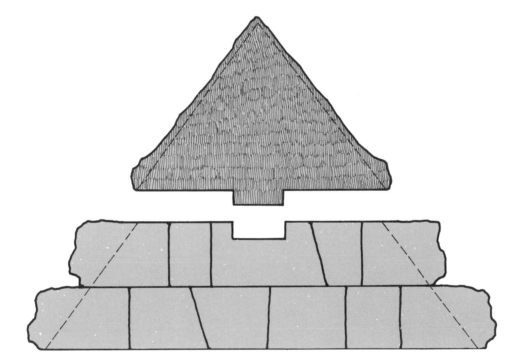

Once the sled was in place the capstone was raised onto wooden blocking. The sled was then removed and the blocking carefully pulled out. A piece of stone that protruded from the base of the capstone slipped snuggly into a hole cut in the center of the last course. This made the bond more permanent and guaranteed that the capstone was directly over the center of the pyramid.

As the last piece of blocking was removed the capstone sat firmly on its base and the actual building of the pyramid was finished. In gratitude, the priests standing on the ramps around the capstone burned incense and offered prayers to the gods.

At the completion of the ceremonies, laborers began dismantling the remaining construction ramps. When they had removed about thirty feet of the rubble and mud another gang erected wooden scaffolding to support work platforms around the exposed portion of the pyramid. From the highest platform workmen using pieces of stone and abrasive powder ground the capstone into a smooth shining peak. Below them other workers chiseled away the steps of the casing, after which that area was also ground and polished. When work on the upper portion of the casing was complete thirty more feet of each ramp was removed and the scaffolding reconstructed at a lower level. This process was repeated until the entire surface of the pyramid was finished.

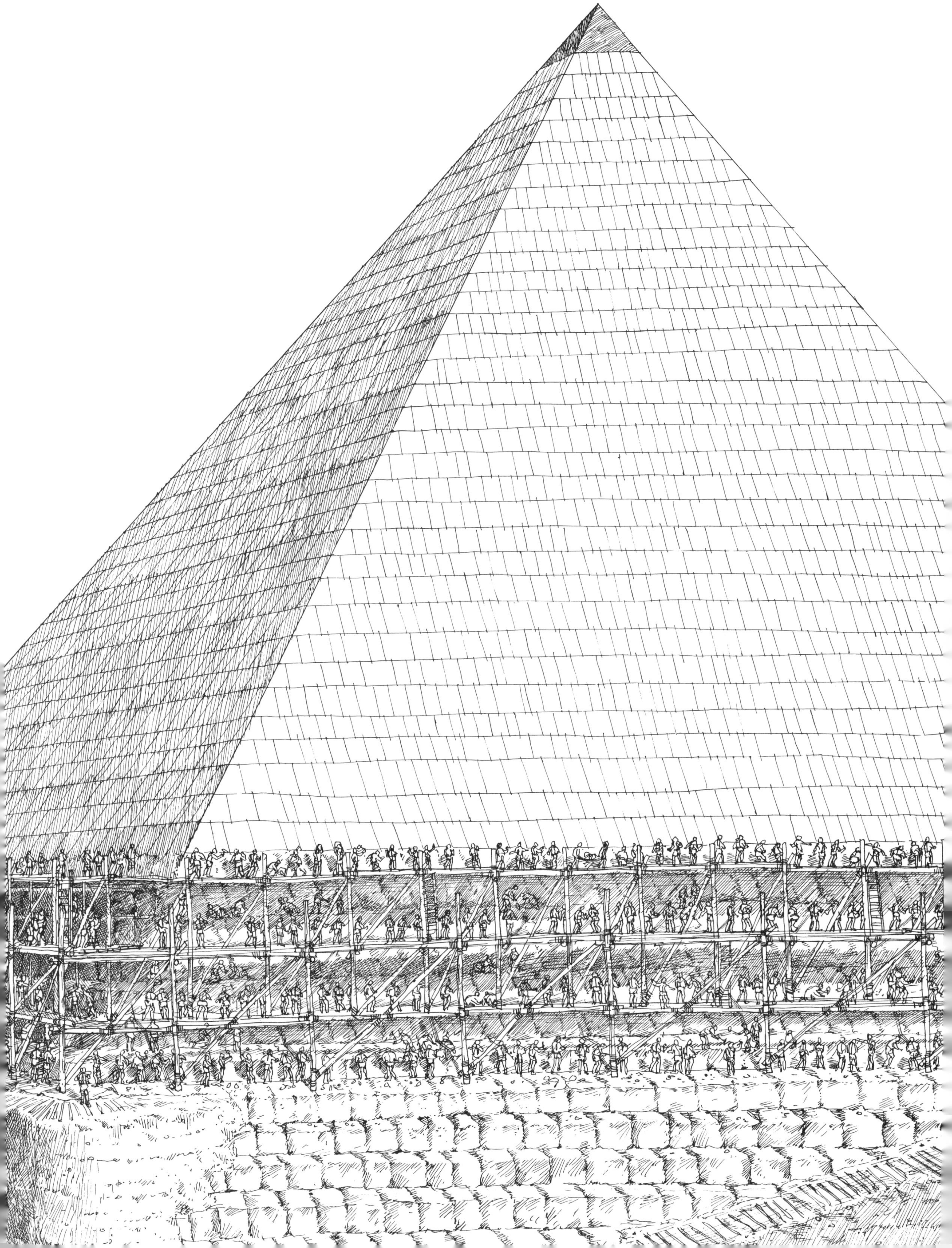

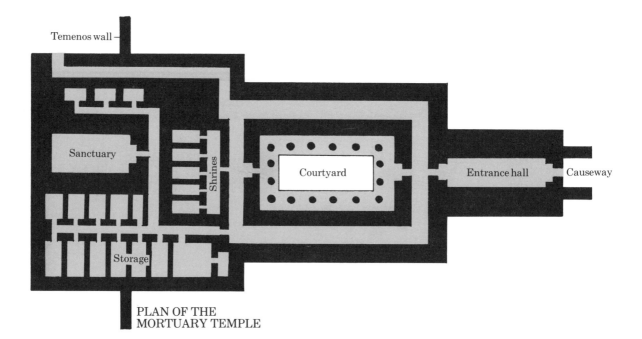

Temenos wall

Sanctuary

Shrines

Courtyard

Entrance hall

Causeway

Storage

PLAN OF THE
MORTUARY TEMPLE

By the time the capstone was in place the stone for the temples and causeway had been delivered and cut to size.

The mortuary temple was finished first. It contained an entry hall, a large open courtyard, five shrines, the sanctuary with its false door, and several storage rooms. A passage led from the courtyard to a thirty-foot-wide area around the base of the pyramid which was enclosed by the high temenos wall. When the first course of the temple had been laid, the enclosed area was filled with earth. The stones of the second course were dragged up a ramp outside the building, across the fill and into place. More earth was then piled up to the top of the new blocks. When the core walls were complete, the earth, which now filled the entire temple, was dug out and the process repeated to construct the facing.

When that fill was removed roughly cut granite columns were erected to support the roof. Each shaft was hoisted into place by gangs of workmen pulling on ropes from the tops of the walls. Other men guided the columns from behind with levers. When all the columns were in place the temple was again filled and the roof slabs hauled up the ramp into position.

When the roof was completed the fill was removed layer by layer. It served as a platform from which skilled workers carved and then painted on the facing stones scenes of the pharaoh's journey into the next life. At the same time others finished the capitals on top of the columns. The floor was finished last. It was paved with finely cut alabaster slabs.

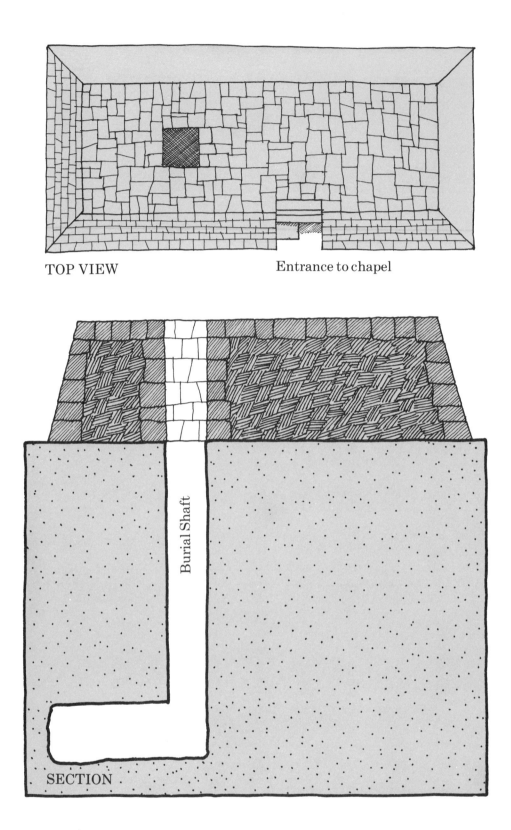

TOP VIEW

Entrance to chapel

Burial Shaft

SECTION

While the temples were under construction, mastabas (tombs) were built along narrow streets laid out around the royal buildings. They were owned by the more important members of the pharaoh's court, and one of the largest belonged to Mahnud Hotep. They were flat-roofed rectangular structures with sloping

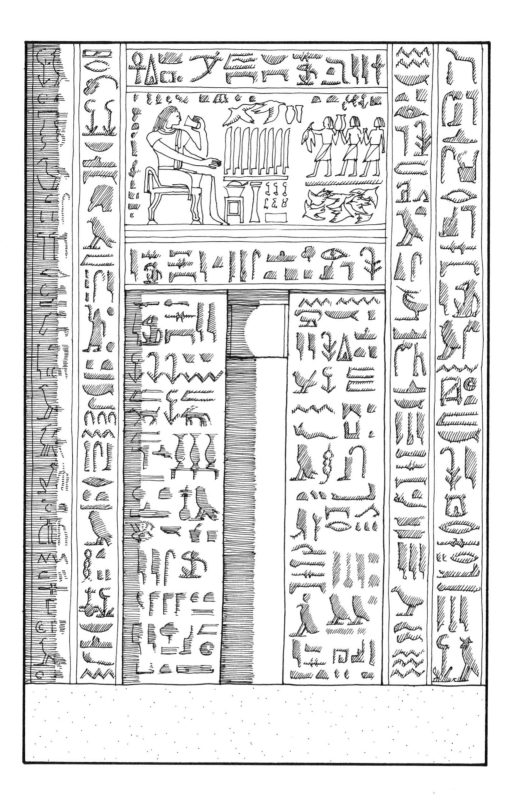

walls. The bodies were placed in a chamber at the bottom of a deep shaft cut in the rock below the mastaba. Each tomb contained a statue of the deceased to which the ka would occasionally return and a chapel where offerings were made. The false door was located on the west wall of the chapel.

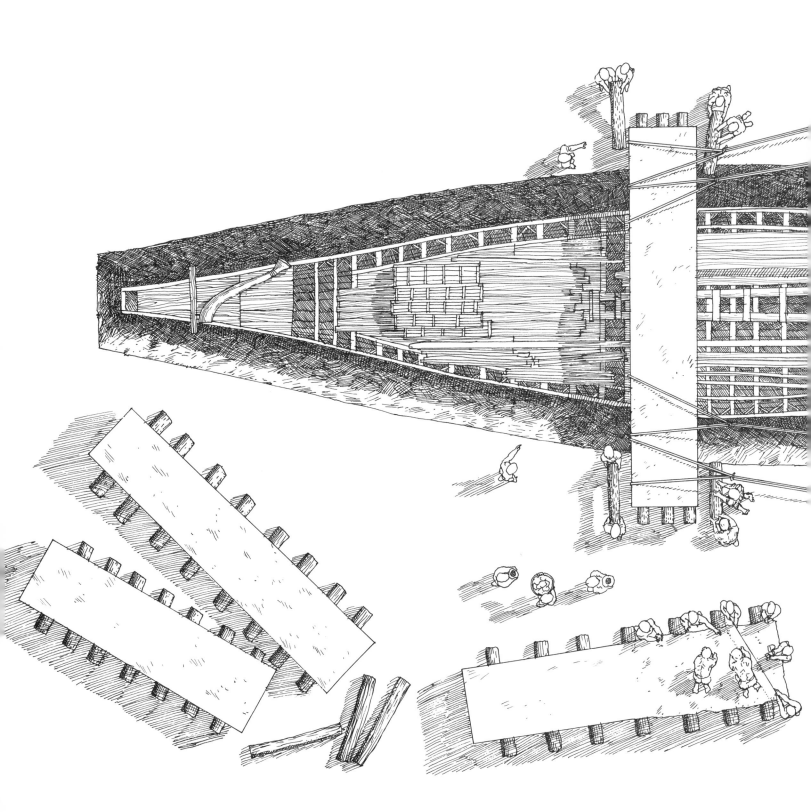

When the mortuary temple was finished, oblong pits were cut into the rock along both sides. Boats specially constructed for the pharaoh's use in the next

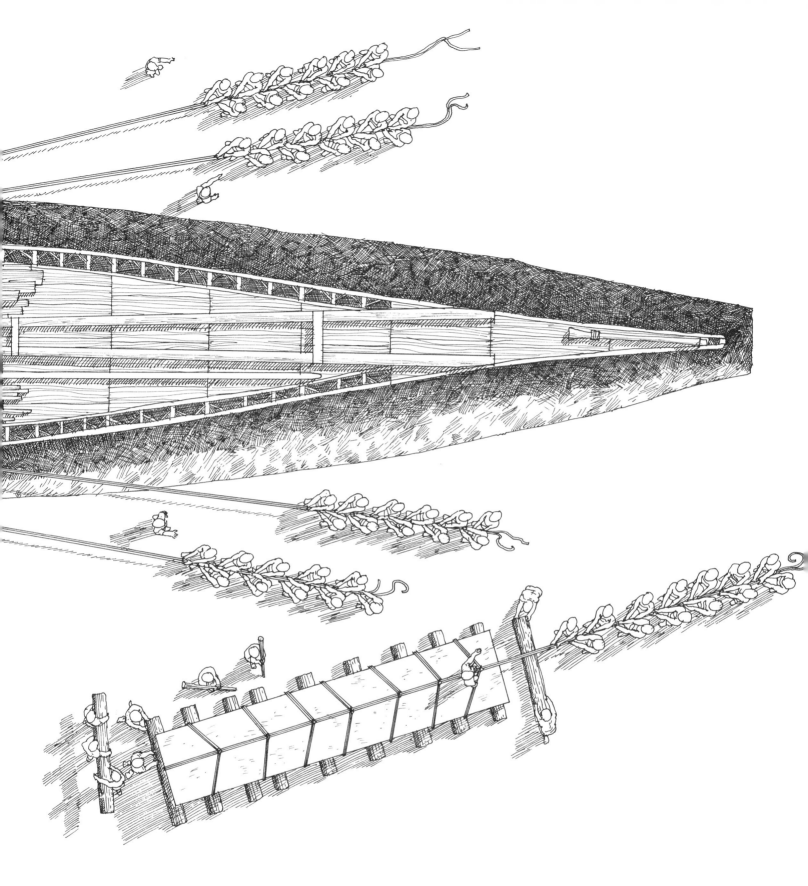

world were placed in five of the six pits. Each pit was then covered with several carefully fitted stone slabs whose seams were coated with plaster.

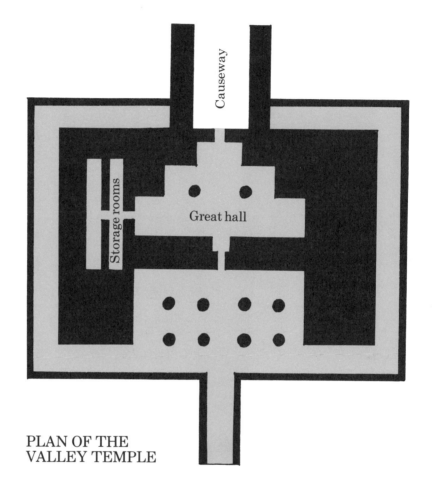

PLAN OF THE
VALLEY TEMPLE

The causeway was completed next. Like the mortuary temple, the walls were constructed first and then the roof slabs dragged across the fill and into place. The interior passage was eight feet wide and ten feet high and illuminated by slots cut in the roof. The walls were covered with painted relief carvings depicting some of the pharaoh's more impressive deeds — both real and imaginary.

The valley temple was constructed in exactly the same way as the mortuary temple and was the last to be finished. It contained a large impressive hall and several small storage rooms. Several stone statues of the pharaoh carved in the royal workshop near the pyramid were positioned around the great hall. Laborers were still laying the alabaster floor slabs when, in the spring of 2439, the pharaoh died.

His body was placed on the royal funerary barge in preparation for his last journey on earth. Thousands of people lined the river as the procession sailed by. Another boat carried relatives, including the queen and the pharaoh's son and successor. Others brought close friends and professional mourners. The high priests were waiting as the boats approached the valley temple. When the body had been removed, the royal barge was carefully dismantled and placed in the last of the pits.

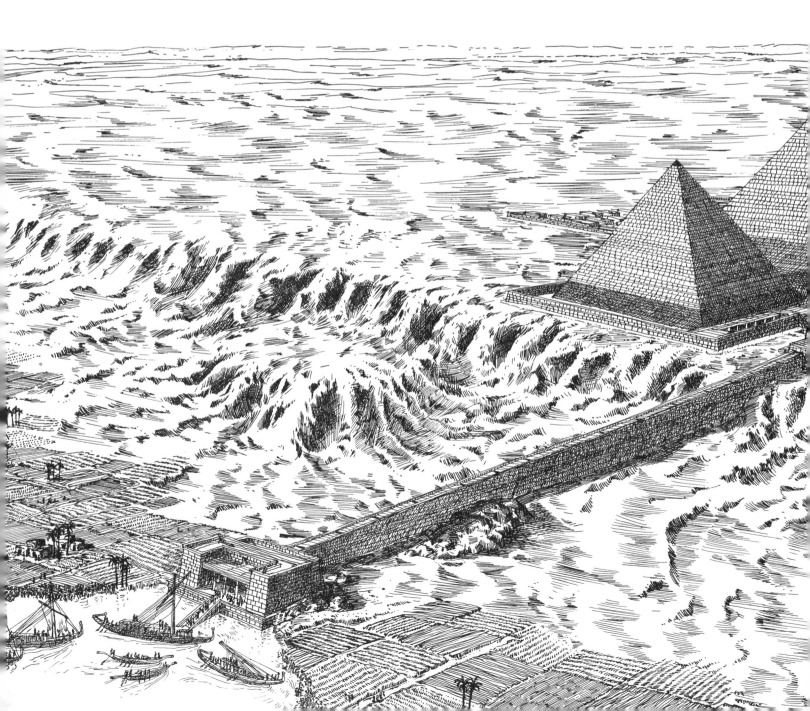

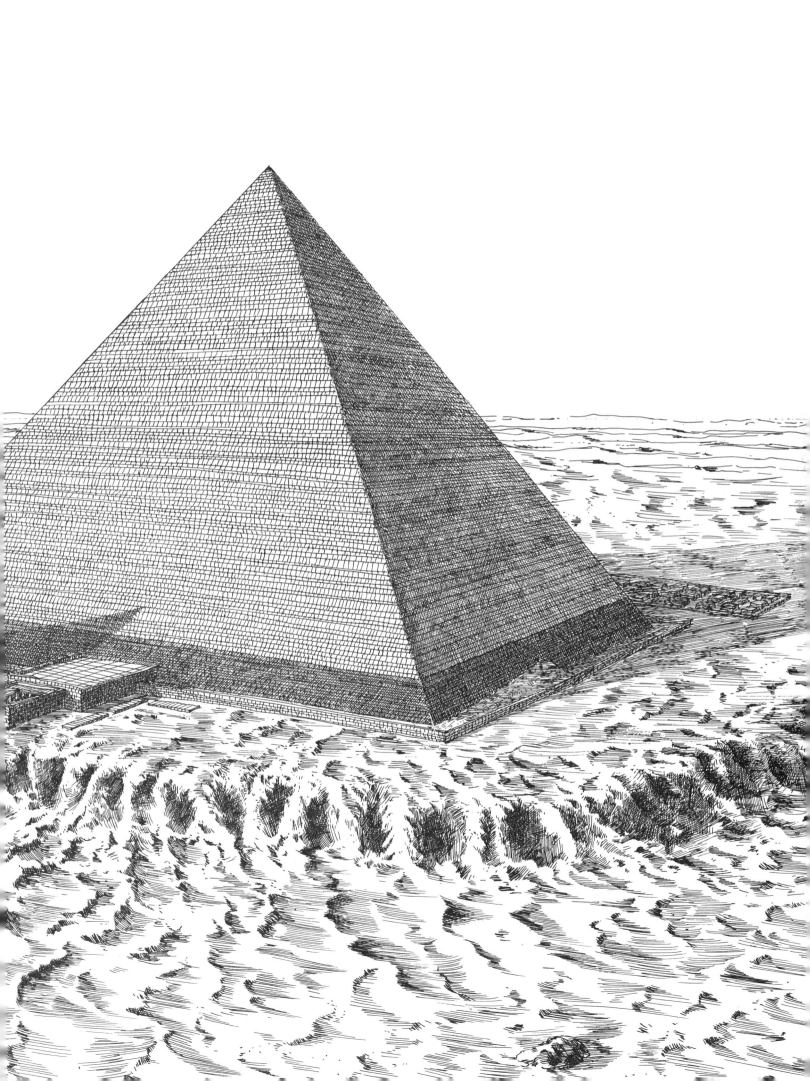

Preparing the pharaoh's body for burial was a complicated procedure taking well over two months. Above all, the body had to be well preserved and for this reason it was mummified. Each step of the process was accompanied by the appropriate religious ceremonies. The corpse was first taken to the embalmers' workshop located near the valley temple.

It was laid out on a large table around which the priests could work. First the brain, having been dissolved with a special liquid, was removed through the nose with small hooks. Then the liver, lungs, stomach, and intestines were removed through a slit along the left side of the body. Each was embalmed and placed in a container called a canopic jar. The heart was left in place. After being dried in salt and washed the body was anointed with ointments and covered with resins. The purified body was then wrapped in alternating layers of linen sheets and bandages. Religious ornaments made of gold and precious stones were placed between every few layers and the body was covered with more resin.

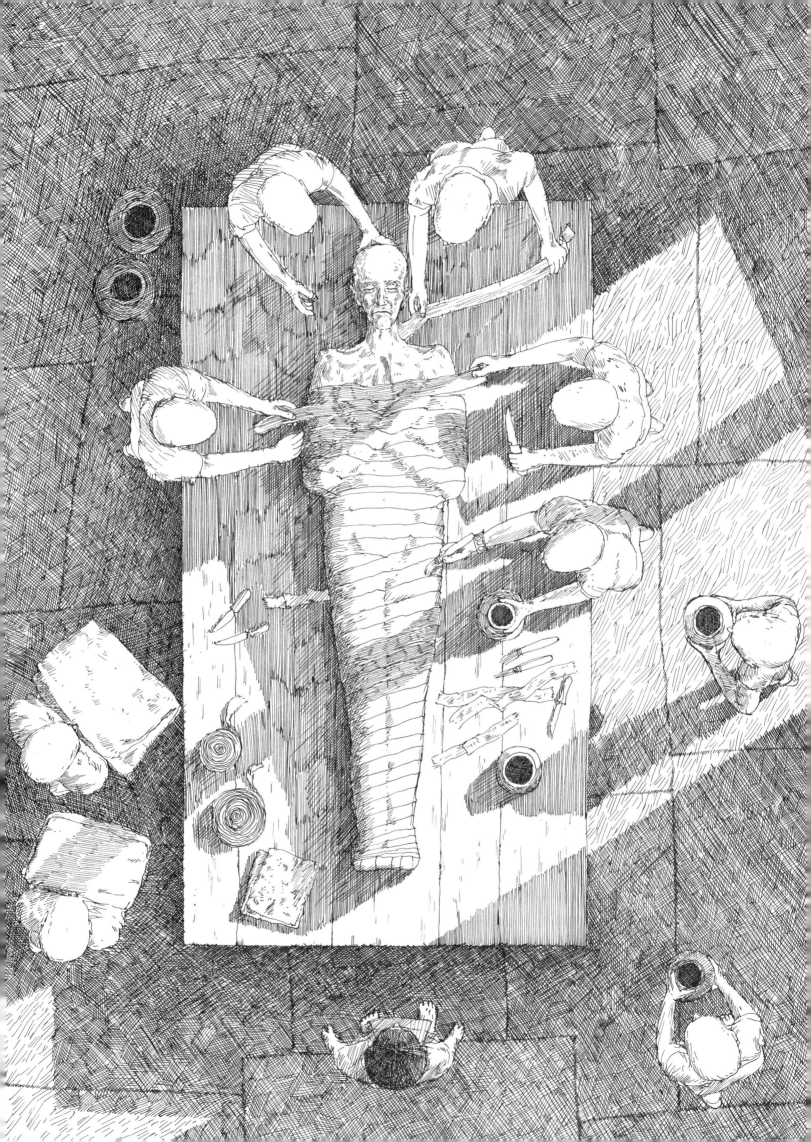

When the mummy was finished it was taken to the large hall of the valley temple where a ceremony called "opening the mouth" was performed. Although the mouth was not actually opened, the ceremony symbolically restored to the pharaoh his ability to eat, speak, and move — all of which were necessary in the next life.

Several days later the mummy was placed in a wooden coffin and taken up the causeway into the courtyard of the mortuary temple. Following more prayers and offerings, it was placed on an elaborate sled and dragged up a temporary ramp built between the north side of the pyramid and the temenos wall.

From the entrance to the tunnel the coffin was carried by the priests into the burial chamber. It was lowered into the sarcophagus which was in turn covered by a heavy granite lid. The four canopic jars were then placed in a wooden box at the foot of the sarcophagus. The rest of the chamber and the storeroom were filled with those objects used by the king during his life which were believed necessary in the afterlife. They included food, clothing, furniture, jewelry, weapons, and even games to occupy the slow moments of eternal life.

After blessing the tomb and its occupant for the last time, the priests left the pyramid, lowering the portcullises behind them. Then several granite blocks were slipped one by one into the tunnel. Mahnud Hotep himself supervised the final ceremony as the last casing stone was pushed into the remaining space to conceal the entrance forever.

With the removal of the ramp the pharaoh's eternal home was finished. His sacred body lay protected under a perfect manmade mountain of more than two million blocks of stone.

GLOSSARY

ALABASTER
A very fine stone through which light can be seen.

BA
A person's soul which was believed to live on earth after death, resting within the body at night.

BONING RODS
A set of three wooden rods, two of which are connected by a string from the tops. The rods are placed vertically on opposite sides of the area of the stone which is to be cut and the string pulled taut. The third rod is slid vertically under or next to the string, rising above it when part of the stone is higher than the rest. That area can then be chiseled down.

CANOPIC JAR
The container in which one of the organs from the corpse was placed after being embalmed.

CAPITALS
The ornate topmost part of the columns on which the roof beams rest.

CAPSTONE
The pyramid-shaped stone on the top of the pyramid.

CASING BLOCKS
The outermost stones of the pyramid, which were highly polished.

CAUSEWAY
The covered passage which connects the Valley Temple to the Mortuary Temple.

CORE BLOCKS
Those blocks that create the central core of the pyramid.

DOLERITE
A very hard stone used for pounding through granite and limestone.

EMBALMING
The treating of a corpse with preservatives to prevent or slow down the deterioration process.

FUNERARY COMPLEX
A group of related tombs and temples constructed on the west bank of the Nile for the burial and worship of the dead.

INUNDATION
The time between July and November when every year the Nile flooded the farmland along its banks.

KA
The spiritual duplicate of a person which after death traveled back and forth between the land of the living and the land of the dead.

MASTABA
The rectangular tomb structure with sloping walls containing a chapel for offerings and a small chamber for a statue of the deceased who was buried at the bottom of a vertical shaft cut directly below.

MORTAR
A mixture of sand, lime, and water used mostly as a lubricant on which the heavy blocks of stone could be more easily moved.

MORTUARY TEMPLE
The temple closest to the pyramid in which certain ceremonies were performed before the body of the pharaoh was taken into the pyramid. This temple also served as the home of the Ka.

MUMMIFICATION
The process of embalming and preserving a dead body and its vital organs.

PACKING BLOCKS
Blocks placed on the steps of the core on which the casing stones are then placed.

PHARAOH
An Egyptian king.

PLUMBLINE
A weighted string which because of gravity will always hang perfectly vertical.

PORTCULLISES
The granite slabs that were lowered between two grooves to seal the entrance to the tomb after the pharaoh's burial.

RESIN
A substance obtained from plants and used to coat the corpse to prevent decomposition.

ROCKER
A wooden frame on which a block of stone was placed before being finished so that it could be more easily moved around.

SARCOPHAGUS
The stone coffin in which the wooden coffin containing the pharaoh's mummy was placed.

TEMENOS WALL
The thirty-foot-high wall built around the base of the pyramid. These walls were originally built around entire funerary complexes.

VALLEY TEMPLE
The temple on the banks of the Nile to which the body of the pharaoh was first brought.